Strategies of Persecution

John D King 

ISBN -13:978-0692249611
ISBN – 10:0692249613

Dedication

I dedicate this book to our team members in this Men's Ministry, The Bridgeport Book Club and Talk Group for Men would like to thank you for your help, support and service on this side of the vineyard.

Contents

Acknowledgments

I would like to thank my lord Jesus for making all this possible for me without him this book would not be possible. For my mom who loved me from the start Elaine King the best mother anyone can have, to my wife for standing with me in my good times and bad times, to my family everyone that helped me on my way, to my church home and all the people of God that are praying for me thank you, loving everyone no matter what. To all those who kept me in your prayers thank you.

And the lord God formed man of the dust of the ground, and breathed into his nostrils the breath of life, and man became a living soul

Genesis 2:7 KJV

When man was formed, strategies of life was formed in the man, strategies to live in the will of God. Adam mastered all the strategies God placed in him, everything Adam was given came from the breath of God. What we have today came from the breath of God, the way we smell, think, speak, hear and the things we see. They are foundations of strategies, but the greatest of them is smell, God breathed into his nostrils the breath of life. How we smell is what keeps us today, it allows us to be a living soul. The enemy don't want us to understand the breath of life, the spirit of God that brings intelligent life.

The enemy's Strategies is to keep us from The Breath of life, the spirit of God

We as men and women live many lives

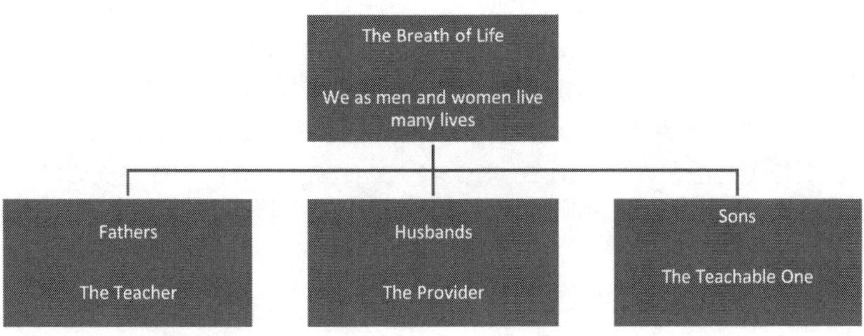

Communication

Have you ever been in a place where people have been applauding your down fall?

Have you ever been hated for being honest?

Has wisdom ever landed you over people that hate you?

Do you know that Satan uses Strategies to bring you down?

Why some are hated when they walk the path of Jesus Christ?

Are you a believer or a doubter?

Let's open to spiritual thinking, Gods way of thinking, then we will understand more of the enemies' strategies. A lot of Christians are hated when they walk the path that Jesus Christ has purposed for their lives.

Here we have the believer and the doubter, the believer sees promise and hears promise. The doubter allows his mind to be a playing field for the enemy.

Do you know believers can?
   1. See Gods Promises

   2. Hear Gods Promises

   3. Touch Gods Promises

God will allow you to see, hear and touch the beginning and the end. This is a privilege for the believer, the doubter will always have the same privilege, but he must believe he can open that door called promise.

The believer lives a life in two systems.

1. **The Natural System
What we see with our eyes is the natural system.**

2. **The Spiritual System
It is a heavenly realm consisting of the things of God.**

The Systems walk hand and hand, but never over lapping and never connecting but one knowing the other exists. I asked myself, how then can we move in this life as natural and spiritual beings. When I see the natural things in life some of them I can control, my surroundings allow me to open my mind and take part in what has been placed in me. God's promises take hold, but His will is my foundation.

When I read my bible and study God's word I see things in the spirit as I open my heart to the Holy Ghost.

- ✓ **Seeing Spiritual-** opens doors to spiritual Worship.
- ✓ **Seeing Natural-** opens doors to Natural Worship.

So, what does that tell me, that my Natural Worship can only take me but so far? Jesus said he that worship, must worship, in spirit and in truth.

Humanity has been given an inheritance called worship.

The spiritual Worship gives us the power to overcome all spiritual attacks.

For God hath not given us the spirit of fear; but of power, and of love, and of a sound mind
2 Timothy 1:7 KJV

The Natural Worship gives us the power to overtake and to have power over the things of this world, given God thanks for all that we have. This will be the beginning of natural worship.

Forward

The Emphasis of God
Seen in Adam

Inherited Power- it's God word filled with the promises of God. The level of our inheritance that is seen in a spiritual sense which is heard and touched.

- **Seeing Promise**

- **Hearing Promise**

- **Touching Promise**

Worship Power- the worship that comes out of us always attached to us with the three promises, this power is always bring increased by God.

Spiritual Power- the platform that was planted under the feet which always increases so that there is a relationship with God on every spiritual level of our walk with God. It renews itself when he moves forward not backwards.

The power that we inherit helps us recognize most of the times we are attacked by the enemy. He uses Strategies to distract us from or inheritance.

Inherit Power

Touching Promise- We find that Adam's inherited power gave him the will and power to till the ground, also the willing mind set to fasten seeds, and the power forms them to pullout of themselves.

Seeing Promise- the caring out of God's purpose, landed Adam into seeing promise, the pull out of the characters of the Animals which gave them promise. By giving them names and seeing what was in them, that power gave Adam authority.

And out of the ground the LORD God formed every beast of the field, and every fowl of the air; and brought them unto Adam to see what he would call them; and whatsoever Adam called every living creature, that was the name thereof

Genesis 2:19 KJV

Hearing Promise- God wanted to see what he would do with his inheritance and the level of obedience Adam was on. He was the first human thinker to hear and think, also speak it to pass. Adam had the power to pull out of what he was placed over. **On what level is your pull?**

And God said, let us make man in our image, after our likeness: and let them have dominion over the fish of the sea, and over the fowl of the air, and over the cattle, and over all the earth, and over every creeping thing that creepeth upon the earth.

Genesis 1:26 KJV

The Inherited Power was placed in him by when God blows the breath of life in Adam.

And the LORD God formed man of the dust of the ground, and breathed into his nostrils the breath of life; and man became a living soul.

Genesis 2:7 KJV

Worship Power- God gave Adam the power of worship not just with his mouth but his hands; it was his most important thing to bring forth his worship to God.

God gives us gifts of worship we can always give it back to him with our worship, when we do this action with or hearts it becomes a very powerful worship that we can be fruitful and multiply and replenish the earth and subdue it and have dominion over it.

And God blessed them, and God said unto them, Be fruitful, and multiply, and replenish the earth, and subdue it: and have dominion over the fish of the sea, and over the fowl of the air, and over every living thing that moveth upon the earth.

Genesis 1:28 KJV

This Command given by God has a spiritual meaning. By walking and living a spiritual life and in obedience, it will also land you into the power, and loving peace and grace of God. (Five is the number of grace) All five will open the windows of haven.

This is a feeding by God. It places your spirit in a land of Abundance. God provides Spiritual and Natural food for us. His voice gave Adam spiritual food and allowed everything to yield to his words also the seeds of the ground. The platform that was created and first planed in the ground is now planted in him.

Adam landed in an abundant place. He had authority over all things and it empowered him to have many streams of abundance.

Do you have streams of income?

And God said, behold, I have given you every herb bearing seed, which is upon the face of all the earth, and every tree, in the which is the fruit of a tree yielding seed; to you it shall be for meat.

And to every beast of the earth, and to every fowl of the air, and to every thing that creepeth upon the earth, wherein there is life, I have given every green herb for meat: and it was so.

And God saw every thing that he had made, and, behold, it was very good. And the evening and morning were the sixth day.

Genesis 1:29-31 KJV

Strategies of Persecution

Strategies of Persecution

Chapter 1

Adversary / Enemy

Have you ever been in a place where it seemed like the world was holding you from operating on a higher level of your calling? The gravity of life was holding you back from flying over the mountains of hard times.

The Adversary uses strategies to release persecution on the people of God; most of the time it's to distract you from your calling and to kill your purpose and worship holding you down, his job is to bind you from a spiritual life. Satan is always cheering on the flesh, so that you can fall into sin.

When you are a believer, God is in you and you in God, the attack come in two dimensions, (Adversary and Enemy). Persecution comes from the outside, but God's grace, mercy and peace (Holy Spirit) is on the inside helping you fight of the outside attack.

Enemy – he is a foe of all righteousness, when we strive to live a life of peace, love, holiness and the things of God. the enemy has now targeted you to distract us from Gods best in our lives, not just to block us but to bind everything we are and what God has for us.

We see the enemy's strategies every day, they are traps that are in our pathways every day, some distractions are to hold us in bondage, some are to tear us away from our gifts. Most of the time they are to hold us from our purposes, some are to take us off that path of righteousness. Many times, he will come the same way. Why most of us fall for the same strategies?

Satan knows our past and our up's and down's that is how he decides his strategies of attack on us, he also uses or past to build his ongoing nuisance to release persecution on the people of God. most of the time it is something from or past, many of us walk the same steps every day. Satan knows your old ways of living.

The one thing I love is that the bible says that our steps are ordered by the Lord. When God orders our steps, the enemy can't find us, Adams steps were ordered by God that is why Satan could not find him in the garden. However, in the garden his wife had a conversion with the enemy, I believe Adam was so spiritual that he couldn't speak to what was flesh (he never said a word to the enemy only his wife spoke. The strategy is to keep you rolling over and over, "Did God really say".

Do you know yourself?

Many times, I find myself in a place where I find myself studying my own ways, seeing if my ways line up with the word of God, that through him I my become a mighty God-fearing man in his sight, not in the sight of man but to be effective with man.

Understanding the intellects of a person who they are and what they represent and in themselves we can understand the more. It is plainly seen in their walk with God.

Walk- a man's life style is introduced in his actions, understanding the intellects of a person can also be heard verbally, most of the time it is plainly heard what they are standing for.

By a person actions that is who he or she is, without God he or she has no real spiritual movement the actions of life are dead and there is no spiritual profit, there is only earthly gain. Without God there is no straight path.

Why do we seek after him when it is dark?

When we are trapped in a place, where the way out is not in our site and we can't see our hands in front of our face, why do some of us wait so long to call on Jesus? A wise woman said always keep Jesus on the tip of your mouth. I was always told actions speak louder than words. A person's actions can almost determine who he or she is, the mind releases verbally into places knowing that it is proclaimed in his speech.

That they should seek the lord, if haply they might feel after him, and find him, though he be not far from every one of us:
For in him we live, and move, and have our being; as certain also of your own poets have said, for we are also his offspring.
Forasmuch then as we are the offspring of God, we ought not to think that the Godhead is like unto gold, or silver, or stone, graven by art and man's device.

Acts 17:27-29 KJV

Do you know your own actions can be used to attack you? It can be used as strategies to make you stumble in life. Would God be happy with your walk and the way you talk with people?

Many of us live our life in a certain way. Can I look at your actions and see a Godly person? Many people don't see their own actions most of the time it's like what I do doesn't matter if any one sees me do it. Some men and women of God my look like the move of God is all over them on the outer shell, but don't judge them pray for them, God is working on the inner person so when the inner is complete it will become one with your outer actions.

Walk = Action = Testimony

Talk = Speech = Power

Our walk-in life and the trials and roads we take brings forth a testimony that is picked up by our actions.

Your actions are how you get there and back. How you handle the situation that comes into your life.

Do you know your talk is who you are; your mind speech is where you are going. The power that comes out is only given to you when the Holy Spirit is in your vocal cords. That's way your breath brings and moves your life.

And Saul was consenting unto his death. And at that time there was a great persecution against the church which was at Jerusalem; and they were all scattered abroad throughout the regions of Judaea and Samaria, except the apostles.

And devout men carried Stephen to his burial, and made great lamentation over him.

As for Saul, he made havock of the church, entering into every house, and haling men and women committed them to prison.

Therefore they that were scattered abroad went every where preaching the word.

Act 8:1-4 KJV

Saul was cheering on the deaf of Stephen, placing fear in the hearts of the people of God, there was great persecution on the church, the strategies was to hold the church from Kingdom Work. Saul tried to bind up the homes and keep the men from the kitchen table, the teaching table. The strategies were to destroy the unity of the house hold by haling men and women to prison.

Chapter 2

Prediction

Do we walk with the same action or movements?

Can I predict your way of thinking?

Stephens deaf was a strategy to dismantle the gospel of Jesus Christ. Satan wanted to stop what was planted in the heart of Stephen a man full of the Holy Ghost and wisdom. He was a man appointed by the people and of honest report, a man of God who had a powerful life, a back-ground life, he was a man just like me.

The bible called Stephen a man of honest report; he did not waver in his work for God. Satan plan was to bring up his past to stop him in his heart, love and joy to destroy his peace. But what Stephen had was in his spirit, he was full of the Holy Ghost and wisdom. (Acts 6:3) Stephen was a witness, a walking testimony. If you are a walking testimony, the enemy is going to use persecution to make you look bad wherever you go, his strategy is to make your testimonies look like a lie that God is not working thinks out in your life.

Man, of God, women of God, don't let your walk be in vain, don't stop living out your testimonies but keep standing.

Chapter 3

Spiritual Wounds

As I began to meditate on this lesson and the strategies of the adversary, most of the time we are attacked by the things because of who we've become and what we have done by knowing our past. Many times, it's things that we have done or attempted to do, we find it on different levels or in an oversight form what we may think. Sometimes it's from our own actions, outlined by our own flesh and what we allow our flesh to engage in trying to delete Jesus from our lives.

Do you know, no matter who isn't on my side or how many strategies the enemy uses to attack us. My wife is always there to pray for me, to encourage me and speak life into my spirit, she knows how to mend spiritual wounds, the grace and mercy in her words that comes from God to her for me, and the wisdom to help strengthen my leadership walk.

The enemy uses the things we fight with in our everyday way of living, knowing and trying to bind our spirits with unclean things.

The adversary cheers on the flesh from the outside. Have you ever been in a place where your surrounding tries to overwhelm you with your actions, holding you bound to what comes from the outside. When I began to open the lessons and dig into the word of God things started to happen around me. This assessment was given to me by God, the attacks I faced where to try and keep me from writing this book. A distraction came my way, but the strategy was to stop my ten lessons from coming forward.

Saul was consenting onto Stephen death, the enemy pushes the flesh to stop you from standing for God, by approving our flesh to fall cheering on from behind.

The adversary uses distraction to keep us in a wondering state of thinking, keeping us from that appointed time and place to move us off the path of holiness. Many times, the attributes of the world is what keeps us moving around and around to bind us. What we see here is called a power play to procrastination, a strategy to keep us standing still.

Chapter 4

Power Play Strategies

The adversary uses distraction to keep us in a wondering state of mind and to keep us from our appointed time, to move us off that path of holiness. Many times, the attributes of this world is what keeps us moving in a path that looks Godly, but the end is deaf. What we see here is what I call a power play from the enemy to keep us standing still.

Procrastination

Everything you do stop trying to please man but work please God so the he can use you to be effective with man. Many times, some of us are wavering up and down in and out in our minds, step out, stop procrastinating and jump. One day they are with you cheering you on and the next day they are nailing you to a cross. Brother and sister don't hesitate in your walk, if God says move then step out and walk, set your mind on higher things.

Let's Talk procrastination, it can delay your time or even stop you from walking in that door called purpose. The enemy uses many kinds of strategies, one of them is called rejection to make you lose your faith so that you can tell yourself I can't do it, or he doesn't like me, or she doesn't care for me. Don't turn away from rejection it will bring on procrastination, keep walking toward God and his purpose.

And whatsoever ye do, do it heartily, as to the lord, and not unto men;
Knowing that of the lord ye shall receive the reward of the inheritance: for ye serve the lord Christ

Colossians 3:23-24 KJV

Thank you for reading this book, God has plans for you to push his word more in your reading, hope you enjoy God Bless.

Strategies of Persecution

Made in the USA
Monee, IL
08 July 2026

56679415R00026